Lerner SPORTS

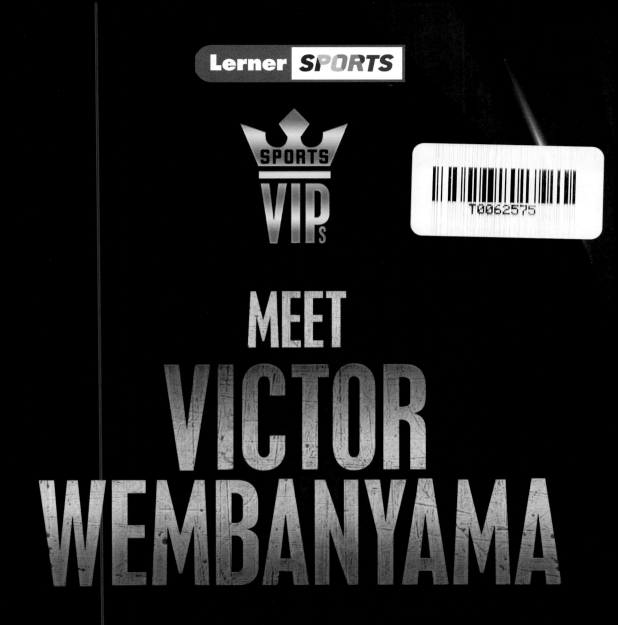

SPORTS
VIPs

MEET VICTOR WEMBANYAMA

MARGARET J. GOLDSTEIN

Lerner Publications ◆ Minneapolis

SPORTS THRILLS MEET RESEARCH SKILLS

Lerner SPORTS

Free Database Trial: **lernersports.com**

Lerner Publications Company
An imprint of Lerner Publishing Group, Inc.
241 First Avenue North
Minneapolis, MN 55401 USA

For reading levels and more information, look up this title at www.lernerbooks.com.

Main body text set in Aptifer Slab LT Pro. Typeface provided by Linotype AG.

Editor: Nicole Berglund

Library of Congress Cataloging-in-Publication Data

Names: Goldstein, Margaret J., author.
Title: Meet Victor Wembanyama : San Antonio Spurs superstar / Margaret J. Goldstein.
Description: Minneapolis : Lerner Publications, [2025] | Series: Sports VIPs (Lerner sports) | Includes
    bibliographical references and index. | Audience: Ages 7–11 years | Audience: Grades 2–3 | Summary: "Power
    forward Victor Wembanyama was the first pick of the NBA draft in 2023, when he signed with the San Antonio
    Spurs. Readers will love exploring the career of this promising young basketball player"— Provided by
    publisher.
Identifiers: LCCN 2023054409 (print) | LCCN 2023054410 (ebook) | ISBN 9798765626030 (lib. bdg.) |
    ISBN 9798765629772 (pbk.) | ISBN 9798765637760 (epub)
Subjects: LCSH: Wembanyama, Victor—Juvenile literature. | Forwards (Basketball)—France—Biography—
    Juvenile literature. | Basketball players—United States—Juvenile literature. | San Antonio Spurs (Basketball
    team)—Juvenile literature. | National Basketball Association—Juvenile literature.
Classification: LCC GV884.W38 G65 2025 (print) | LCC GV884.W38 (ebook) | DDC 796.323092 [B]—dc23/
    eng/20240131

LC record available at https://lccn.loc.gov/2023054409
LC ebook record available at https://lccn.loc.gov/2023054410

Manufactured in the United States of America
1-1010136-51937-2/22/2024

TABLE OF CONTENTS

>>>>>>>>>>>>>>

RISING STAR

The San Antonio Spurs were nervous. They had led the Phoenix Suns by 27 points in the first half. But in the second half of the basketball game, Phoenix had surged back to even the score. With less than four and a half minutes left to play, the score was 116–116. Could San Antonio push ahead for the win?

All eyes turned to Victor Wembanyama, the Spurs' new power forward. Standing 7 feet 4 (2.2 m) and playing in only his fifth NBA game, Wembanyama went into action. In a dizzying few minutes, he scored a three-pointer, three free throws, a dunk, and an 18-foot (5.5 m) jumper. When the buzzer sounded to end the game, the Spurs had 132 points against the Suns' 121.

FAST FACTS

DATE OF BIRTH: January 4, 2004
POSITION: power forward
LEAGUE: National Basketball Association (NBA)

PROFESSIONAL HIGHLIGHTS: joined his first pro team at 15; led the LNB Pro A league in points, rebounds, and blocks in the 2022–2023 season; chosen first in the 2023 NBA draft

PERSONAL HIGHLIGHTS: learned English by watching TV and online videos; loves to read science fiction and fantasy; loves the work of Keith Haring and other artists

Wembanyama (*right*) holds the ball away from Kevin Durant during a game in 2023.

Wembanyama had sealed the win for the Spurs. On top of that, he scored an astounding 38 points in the game. It was no wonder San Antonio had picked him first in the 2023 NBA draft.

Wembanyama could do it all. He hit three-pointers and jump shots with ease. With his great height, he was a supreme shot blocker, rebounder, and dunker. He also had excellent speed and ballhandling skills. NBA superstar LeBron James summed it up: "I've never seen . . . anyone as tall as he is, but as fluid and as graceful as he is out on the floor." Wembanyama began his NBA career in the fall of 2023. The world couldn't wait to see more of him.

Wembanyama attempts a layup in a 2023 game.

FIRST PERIOD

Victor Wembanyama was born January 4, 2004, near Paris, France. He has an older sister, Eve, and a younger brother, Oscar. His mother, Elodie de Fautereau, played pro basketball in France. She taught her three kids how to play. When Victor was young, she coached youth basketball.

Victor joined a boys basketball team when he was seven. He also played soccer and practiced judo. Outside of sports, he loved to draw. One of his favorite artists was Keith Haring. He also enjoyed reading fantasy and science fiction novels.

Wembanyama and his parents, Elodie and Felix

At 10 he joined Nanterre 92. This Paris basketball club has a pro team as well as teams for kids. With Nanterre 92's youth program, Victor improved his dribbling, ballhandling, and other basketball skills. He learned to play all five positions: point guard, shooting guard, small forward, power forward, and center. His dream was to play in the NBA.

Youth teams help kids develop skills.

All the Wembanyamas are athletes. Victor's father, Felix Wembanyama, competed in track and field. His mother played and coached basketball. His grandparents on his mother's side were also basketball players. Victor's sister plays pro basketball in France. His brother may be headed toward a pro basketball career too.

It was easy to spot Victor during his games. He stood out because he was more than a head taller than his teammates. By his early teens, he stood more than 6 feet (1.8 m) tall.

CHAPTER 2

GROWTH SPURT

At Nanterre 92, young players lived together in a dormitory. Their gym and school were close by. Wembanyama moved out of his family home and into the dormitory when he was 14. By then he had grown to 6 feet 11 (2.1 m). Nanterre 92 staff ordered him a longer bed so he could sleep comfortably. They fed him five meals a day to put weight on him.

Playing with Nanterre 92's youth teams, Wembanyama turned heads at games and practices. Coaches and other players were amazed by his basketball skills and his height. Nicolas Batum, a French player for the NBA, saw Wembanyama at a practice. Batum said, "I saw him pick up the basketball and he started dribbling. I was shocked how he could handle the ball at [his] size." Batum called another NBA player to tell him about Wembanyama's skill.

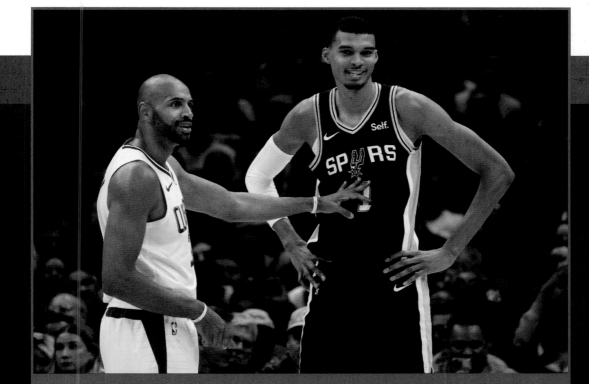

Nicolas Batum (*left*) defends Wembanyama in a 2023 game.

Wembanyama shoots the ball during a 2019 game with Nanterre 92.

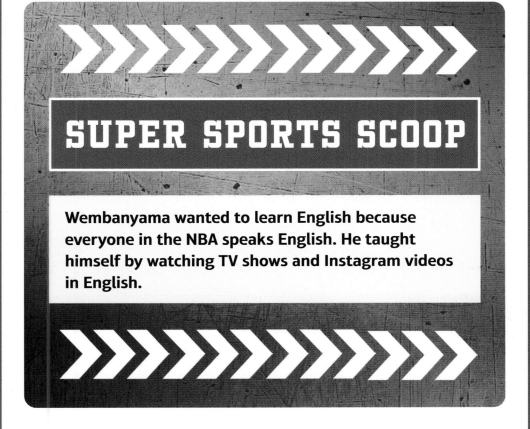

SUPER SPORTS SCOOP

Wembanyama wanted to learn English because everyone in the NBA speaks English. He taught himself by watching TV shows and Instagram videos in English.

Wembanyama was so good that at 15 he joined Nanterre 92's pro team. His teammates were all older and more experienced. That year he also got an agent.

Word of Wembanyama's talent spread far and wide. Michael Bur, one of his Nanterre 92 coaches, said, "Every time there was an event where he was [playing], there was a lot of pressure. . . . All the NBA scouts and everyone was already talking about him."

Wembanyama put up big numbers on the court. In the first game of the Adidas Next Generation Tournament in 2020, he scored 22 points, grabbed 15 rebounds, and made nine blocks. He led his team to a 94–86 victory. By then the 16-year-old stood 7 feet 1 (2.1 m). And he was still growing.

Wembanyama graduated from high school in 2021. That year he switched teams. He signed with ASVEL, part of the French league LNB Pro A and the European EuroLeague. This took him to the highest level of European basketball. He left home to live in Lyon, France, where ASVEL was based.

Wembanyama focuses during a Nanterre 92 game in 2020.

CHAPTER 3

MOVING UP

ASVEL was a strong team, but it didn't suit Wembanyama. The coaches didn't give him a lot of playing time. Torn muscles and other minor injuries also kept him off the court for part of the 2021–2022 season.

Wembanyama blocks a shot during a 2023 game with Mets 92.

Wembanyama looked for another team. He joined Metropolitans 92, based in Paris. Mets 92 wasn't a top team like ASVEL, but it was a good fit for Wembanyama. The coaches gave him lots of playing time. They treated him like a star player. They designed plays and strategies to match his strengths and playing style.

As a power forward and center for Mets 92, Wembanyama did well. He posted big numbers, and the team began to win. Crowds packed into the team's small home arena to see Wembanyama play.

In October 2022, Wembanyama and Mets 92 traveled to a city near Las Vegas, Nevada, to play two exhibition games against NBA G League Ignite. The NBA runs this team to prepare young players for the pro leagues.

Wembanyama in a 2023 Mets 92 game

At the games in Nevada, the stands were filled with NBA insiders eager to see Wembanyama up close. Mets 92 lost the first game and won the second. But in both games, Wembanyama stole the spotlight. In the second game, jaws dropped when Wembanyama blocked a shot and flew to the other end of the court. Then he grabbed an alley-oop from a teammate and scored a slam dunk.

SUPER SPORTS SCOOP

In basketball, a big wingspan is a plus. Having long arms helps players block shots, grab rebounds, steal the ball, and shoot over defenders. Wembanyama's wingspan is 8 feet (2.4 m)—one of the longest ever in the history of basketball.

Wembanyama (*right*) poses with the head of the NBA after the 2023 NBA draft.

Between the two games, he averaged 36.5 points, 7.5 rebounds, and 4.5 blocks. After seeing him in Nevada, basketball experts predicted that Wembanyama would be picked first in the 2023 NBA draft.

Back home in France, Mets 92 played well. During the regular season, the team came in second in its league, LNB Pro A. Wembanyama also led the league in points, rebounds, and blocks. He won many honors, including the league MVP award. Shortly after, he joined the San Antonio Spurs as the number one 2023 NBA draft pick. He was headed to Texas.

CHAPTER 4

ALL EYES ON WEMBY

Wembanyama inked a multimillion-dollar contract with San Antonio. He also signed with Nike to endorse their shoes and other sports gear. He got superstar treatment before playing even one regular-season NBA game. Could he live up to the hype?

In San Antonio, he prepared for his NBA debut. Coaches and trainers wanted him to bulk up so that heavier players couldn't push him around on the court. He ate extra meals and worked out. Over the summer of 2023, he gained 20 pounds (9.1 kg) of muscle.

Durant (*left*) and **Nassir Little** (*right*) block Wembanyama in 2023.

Wembanyama handles the ball.

On October 25, 2023, nearly 19,000 fans and reporters crowded into San Antonio's Frost Bank Center. They were excited to see Wembanyama in his first official NBA game. That night Wembanyama got into foul trouble, which limited his playing time. But in the team's next game against Houston, he showed his greatness.

Fans cheered "Wemby, Wemby" as he dunked, blocked shots, grabbed alley-oops, and jammed the ball through the hoop. He scored 21 points in the overtime win for the Spurs. Excitement soared again on November 2, when Wembanyama worked his magic in a victory over Phoenix.

But that excitement soon turned to frustration. Although Wembanyama still dazzled, his team as a whole struggled. Losses piled up. By the end of December 2023, the Spurs had lost 27 games and won just five.

Wembanyama in 2024

Through it all, Wembanyama remained positive. He predicted that better days were ahead for San Antonio. He told reporters, "Of course, it's hard to be patient sometimes. But it's an everyday fight. I know that the end of the season will not look like the beginning." When asked about losing, he replied, "It just motivates me more.

Fans greet Wembanyama at a press event in 2023.

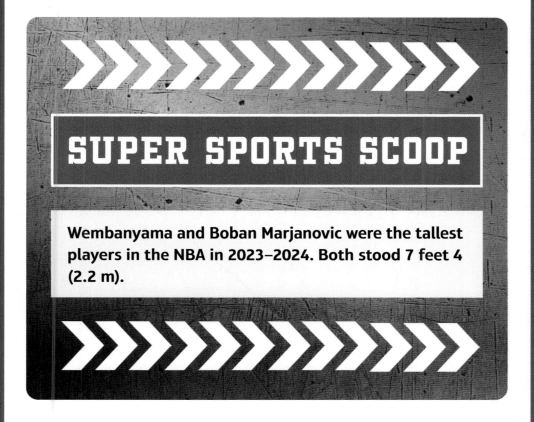

SUPER SPORTS SCOOP

Wembanyama and Boban Marjanovic were the tallest players in the NBA in 2023–2024. Both stood 7 feet 4 (2.2 m).

Nobody in the locker room is putting their head down and giving up. We're not far away [from victory]."

Fans, coaches, and opponents continue to marvel at Wembanyama. His own confidence is sky high. "There's a fire inside of me, a love," he says of his basketball future. "Something that's gonna push me my whole life, I know. I mean, nothing's gonna stop me."

VICTOR WEMBANYAMA
CAREER STATS

GAMES:

35

ASSISTS:

102

POINTS:

694

BLOCKS:

109

REBOUNDS:

355

Stats are accurate through January 2024.

GLOSSARY

agent: a person who manages business deals for a professional athlete

alley-oop: a high pass to a leaping teammate who tries to dunk the ball before landing

center: a player who stays near the basket to grab rebounds and block shots

dormitory: a shared living and sleeping space

draft: a system for choosing new players

endorse: to recommend a product, such as sports gear or clothing, by appearing in ads or using the product in competitions

exhibition game: a game held to show off players' abilities. The outcome does not affect a team's regular-season standings.

forward: a player who focuses on scoring and usually plays near the basket

foul: an action that breaks the rules in a basketball game

guard: a player who focuses on setting up plays and passing the ball

scout: a person who seeks talented athletes for a team or league

wingspan: the distance between one's right and left middle fingers, measured with the arms outstretched

SOURCE NOTES

7 "LeBron James Has High Praise for a Prospect, plus More NBA Quotes of the Week," *ESPN*, October 7, 2022, https://www.espn .com/nba/story/_/id/34742987/lebron-james-high-praise -prospect-plus-more-nba-quotes-week.

13 "Nicolas Batum Reveals Why He Was Shocked by 14-Year-Old Victor Wembanyama," *Basket News*, October 10, 2022, https:// basketnews.com/news-179115-nicolas-batum-reveals-why-he -was-shocked-by-14-year-old-victor-wembanyama.html.

15 Brian Windhorst and Jonathan Givony, "Inside the Decade-Long Plan to Bring Victor Wembanyama to NBA Glory," *ESPN*, May 15, 2023, https://www.espn.com/nba/story/_/id/37651212 /inside-decade-long-plan-bring-victor-wembanyama-nba- glory.

26–27 Michael C. Wright and Michaela Gilmer, "Wemby Watch: Victor Wembanyama Finding Motivation amid Spurs' Losing Skid," NBA, November 19, 2023, https://www.nba.com/news /wemby-watch-victor-wembanyama-nov-19-2023.

27 Jeremy Woo, "Inside Victor Wembanyama's Plan to Dominate the NBA Like Never Before," *Sports Illustrated*, updated May 16, 2023, https://www.si.com/nba/2023/02/21/victor -wembanyama-best-nba-prospect-generation-daily-cover.

LEARN MORE

Fun Basketball Facts for Kids
https://www.sciencekids.co.nz/sciencefacts/sports/basketball.html

Greenberg, Keith Elliot. *LeBron James vs. Michael Jordan: Who Would Win?* Minneapolis: Lerner Publications, 2024.

Lowe, Alexander. *G.O.A.T. Basketball Power Forwards*. Minneapolis: Lerner Publications, 2023.

Moussavi, Sam. *San Antonio Spurs*. New York: Lightbox Learning, 2023.

Sports Illustrated Kids: NBA
https://www.sikids.com/nba

20 Fun Basketball Facts for Kids
https://www.growingplay.com/2023/03/20-fun-basketball-facts-for
-kids/

INDEX

PHOTO ACKNOWLEDGMENTS

Image credits: AP Photo/Darryl Webb, p. 4; Christian Petersen/Getty Images, pp. 6–7, 22, 24; Vibe Images/Shutterstock, p. 8; AP Photo/Nasser Berzane/Abaca/Sipa USA, p. 9; MBI/Alamy, p. 10; Anthony Dibon/Icon Sport/Getty Images, pp. 12, 14, 16, 19; Kevork Djansezian/Getty Images, p. 13; PHILIPPE DESMAZES/AFP/Getty Images, p. 17; AP Photo/Glenn Gervot/Icon Sportswire, p. 18; Sarah Stier/Getty Images, p. 21; Mike Christy/Getty Images, p. 23; AP Photo/Eric Gay, p. 25; AP Photo/Darren Abate, p. 26.

Cover: AP Photo/Darren Abate.